DATE DUE			

LET'S INVESTIGATE SCIENCE
Light and Sound

Peter Lafferty
Illustrated by Terry Hadler

Benchmark Books
MARSHALL CAVENDISH
NEW YORK

Library Edition Published 1996

Benchmark Books
Marshall Cavendish Corporation
99 White Plains Road
Tarrytown, New York 10591-9001

© Marshall Cavendish Corporation 1996

Series created by Graham Beehag Books

Library of Congress Cataloging-in-Publication Data
Lafferty, Peter.
    Light and Sound / by Peter Lafferty
        p. cm. – (Lets investigate science)
    Includes bibliographical references and index.
    Summary: Describes the sources, nature, and behavior of light and sound.
        ISBN 0-7614-0030-3 (lib. bdg.)
    1. Light – Miscellanea – Juvenile literature. 2. Sound –
    Miscellanea – Juvenile literature. [1. Light. 2. Sound.]
    I. Title. II. Series.
    QC360.L34 1996
    535–dc20   95-4465
                                                                       CIP
                                                                        AC

MCC Editorial Consultant: Marvin Tolman, Ed.D.
                    Brigham Young University

Printed in Hong Kong

Contents

Introduction 7

Chapter 1
Light 9
Light waves 10
Sources of light 12
Shadows 14
Seeing light 16
Polarized light 18

Chapter 2
Using light 21
Bouncing light 22
Curved mirrors 24
Bending light 26
Lenses 28
Optical instruments 30
Lasers 32

Chapter 3
Light and color 35
Colors 36
Colored objects 38
Mixing colors 40

Chapter 3
Talking music, and noise 43
Making and hearing sounds 44
Measuring sound 46
Bouncing sounds 48
Musical sounds 50
Unpleasent sounds 52
Sound recording 54

Milestones 56
Glossary 57
For Further Reading 61
Answers 62
Index 64

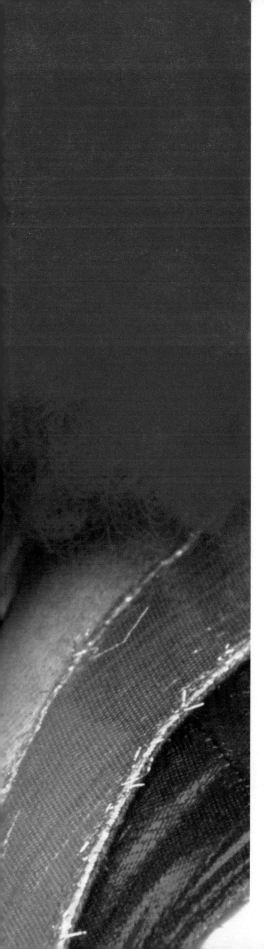

Introduction

Imagine that you are walking through the countryside on a bright summer day. The world seems full of light and color: blue sky, green grass and trees, colored flowers. As you walk, your eyes are using the light to gather information about the world around you. Of all our senses, sight is the most important. About nine-tenths of all the information that reaches our brains comes through our eyes.

On your walk, you can hear many sounds. Your ears are also gathering information. Sound is very important to us because we communicate mainly by talking. When we talk, we use sound to convey our ideas and feelings. We also use light to communicate; when we talk, our facial expressions help other people understand what we mean.

Because sound and light are so much a part of our lives, it is easy to take them for granted. In this book, we will investigate how they are used in our everyday lives, in science, and in industry, to create devices from microscopes and lasers to musical instruments and tape recordings.

Q How much time each day do you spend using your sight (for example, reading, watching television) and how much using your ears (for example, talking, listening to music)?

You can check your answers to the questions featured throughout this book on pages 62-63.

◄ A clown uses light to communicate. The bright colors emphasize his facial expressions, making it easier for him to show gaiety or sadness. He uses sound to communicate, too, by shouting and laughing.

1
Light

◄ **The colors seen in soap bubbles are caused by light waves with different wavelengths (the distance betweeen the wave crests). Each color has a different wavelength.**

What is light? Even today, it is difficult for scientists to answer the question, "What is light?" Scientists agree that light consists of energy that travels through space as waves called electromagnetic waves. This theory explains many of the properties of light. It explains why soap bubbles show colors, for instance. However, there is another theory of light that explains other properties of light.

In the late seventeenth century, the great English scientist Isaac Newton (1642-1727) suggested that a light beam consisted of a stream of tiny particles, which nowadays we call photons. The photons travel in straight lines, so this theory explains the fact that light rays travel in straight lines.

Scientists can't explain how light can be both a wave and a particle. The fact of the matter is that, in some circumstances, light behaves like a stream of particles and, in other circumstances, it behaves like waves.

▼ **Light is a form of energy. Solar power stations convert the energy of sunlight into useful electrical energy. A solar-powered calculator does the same thing, on a smaller scale.**

Light waves

Light and heat energy from the sun is carried across space to the Earth by waves called electromagnetic waves. These waves are ripples of magnetic and electric force produced by the hot material inside the sun. Unlike sound waves, electromagnetic waves do not need air molecules to enable them to travel. In a vacuum, all electromagnetic waves travel at the same speed, 186,000 miles per second (300,000 km per second). This is more than 463,000 times faster than the Concorde supersonic airliner.

Measuring waves

As an electromagnetic wave moves through space, it has a similar shape to ripples on a pond. There is always the same distance between the crests of the wave as they move along. This distance is called the wavelength. The wavelength of an electromagnetic wave is a very small distance, a tiny fraction of an inch or centimeter.

The height of a wave crest or the depth of a trough is called its amplitude. The greater the amplitude of the wave, the more energy it is carrying. The number of wave crests passing

10

The electromagnetic spectrum. The shortest electromagnetic waves are gamma rays. These rays are given out by some radioactive materials, X-rays have wavelengths about 100 times longer than gamma rays. Ultraviolet rays are 100 times longer still. Visible light lies between the ultraviolet and infrared.

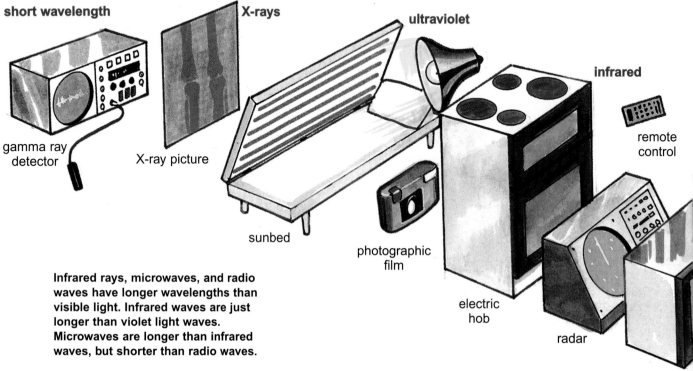

short wavelength

X-rays

ultraviolet

infrared

gamma ray detector

X-ray picture

sunbed

photographic film

remote control

electric hob

radar

Infrared rays, microwaves, and radio waves have longer wavelengths than visible light. Infrared waves are just longer than violet light waves. Microwaves are longer than infrared waves, but shorter than radio waves.

a point in one second is called the frequency of the wave. Frequency is measured in units called hertz; one hertz equals one wave per second.

The electromagnetic family

There is a whole family of electromagnetic waves, each with a different wavelength. The family is called the electromagnetic spectrum. Our senses can detect some of these waves. For example, visible light consists of electromagnetic waves we can see. We can feel other electromagnetic waves as heat rays, called infrared radiation. Most electromagnetic waves are invisible. These include radio waves, microwaves, ultraviolet rays, X-rays, and gamma rays.

The shortest electromagnetic waves, called gamma rays, have a wavelength of less than one-million-millionth of a meter. The longest electromagnetic waves are radio waves. They have a wavelength of several kilometers.

Q If light travels at a speed of 186,000 miles (300,000 km) a second, how far does light travel in one year? This distance is called a light-year. Distances to stars and galaxies are so vast that they are measured in light-years.

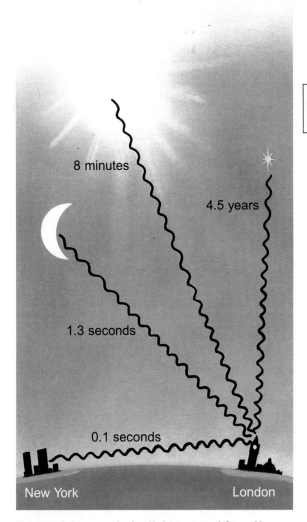

It takes 0.1 seconds for light to travel from New York to London, 1.5 seconds to travel from the Moon to the Earth, eight minutes from the Sun and 4.5 years from the nearest star.

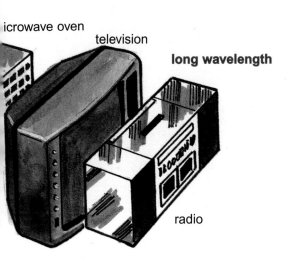

long wavelength

12

INVESTIGATE

Rub an old fluorescent lighting tube with a synthetic cloth such as nylon. The tube will glow when rubbed. You may need to do the experiment in a dark room to see the glow. The rubbing produces an electric field in the tube. This separates some electrons from the gas atoms in the tube. When the electrons fall back into their regular places, they give off light.

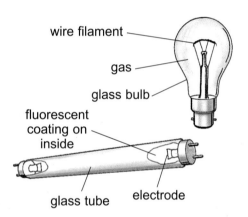

wire filament

gas

glass bulb

fluorescent coating on inside

glass tube   electrode

A light bulb (above top) gives out light when its filament glows. A fluorescent tube (above bottom) contains mercury vapor at low pressure. When electricity passes through the tube, the vapor gives off ultraviolet light, causing the fluorescent coating on the inside of the tube to glow. A discharge tube (right) consists of a tube filled with a gas such as neon. The gas glows when electricity passes through it.

Sources of light

If you closed your eyes, you would not see this page because your eyelids would stop light from entering your eyes. This shows that unless light from an object enters our eyes, we cannot see the object.

Some objects, like the sun, give off their own light. They are called luminous objects. Many luminous objects radiate (give out energy) because they are very hot. They are said to be incandescent. A light bulb is an incandescent source of light. Its filament gets very hot (about 2,500 degrees F) when an electric current is passed through it.

Particles of light

When a material is very hot, its atoms vibrate violently. Charged particles, called electrons, are arranged in layers

inside the atom. From time to time, an electron gains energy because of the atom's vibrations. It jumps from one layer to another, further from the center of the atom. The electron is said to be "excited." After a while, the excited electron falls back to its original position. When this happens, the atom emits light. In this case, we must think of the atom as emitting a particle of light, called a photon.

Direct and indirect light

The light we see directly from a source of light, such as an electric light bulb or a fluorescent lamp, is known as direct light. If this light is reflected or bounced off a surface, the light is known as indirect or reflected light. The light we see from the moon or planets is an example of indirect light. It is the light from the sun that has been reflected by the surface of the moon that reaches our eyes and lets us see the moon.

Q How many luminous objects can you think of?

13

Direct and indirect light. The 'direct light' of the Sun becomes 'indirect light' as it is reflected by a window. The indirect light illuminates an area of shadow that the direct light cannot reach.

Shadows

Light normally travels in straight lines. This simple observation lets us explain why objects have shadows, and why eclipses of the sun and moon occur.

What causes shadows?

Some bodies let light pass through; these materials are called transparent. Some do not allow light to pass through; they are called opaque. Opaque objects cast shadows where they block out the light.

When the source of light is large, such as a light bulb or the Sun, we find that the center of the shadow it casts is dark, This is called the umbra. It is surrounded by an indisinct outer shadow called the penumbra.

14

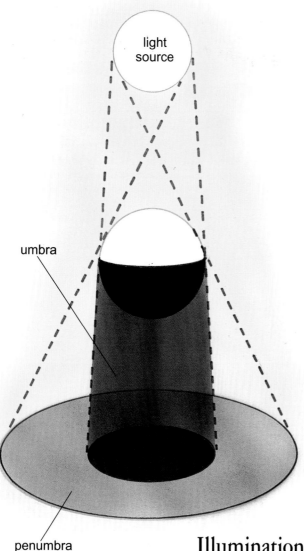

light source

umbra

penumbra

Dark and light shadows

With a large source of light, we often find that shadows have a dark inner region and a lighter outer region. The center or dark shadow is known as the umbra. It occurs because all light rays to this area are blocked out. The lighter outer shadow is known as the penumbra. This occurs because some light can fall in this area.

Eclipses

When the Earth comes between the moon and the sun, it casts a shadow on the moon. When this happens, we first see the moon enter the penumbra and become dimly lit. As it moves into the umbra, the moon is completely blacked out. This is called a lunar eclipse.

When the moon comes between the sun and the Earth, it casts a shadow on the Earth. At points on the Earth lying in the penumbra, the eclipse is partial and the sun is only partly hidden. At points in the umbra, the sun is completely hidden. This is called a total solar eclipse.

Illumination

If you hold this book close to a light, it appears brightly lit.

If you move the book further from the light, it is less brightly lit. This is because less light is falling on the book. The amount of light shining on an object is called the illumination.

The illumination of an object depends upon both the brightness of the light source and distance between the light and the object. The illumination decreases very quickly as the object moves further from a light source.

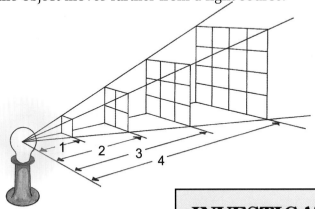

◀ Illumination decreases very fast with distance. The light falling on a square one foot from a light source, is spread over an area four times as large at a distance of 2 feet. Therefore, the illumination of a book 2 feet from a light is one-quarter the illumination at one foot. The illumination decreases as the square of the distance.

15

INVESTIGATE

Cut a disk of cardboard smaller than the size of the lens of a flashlight. Attach the disk to a thin stick. Shine the flashlight onto a wall about 2 feet (60 cm) away. Hold the disk in the beam about 1 foot (30 cm) from the flashlight. What size is the shadow? Repeat the experiment with a disk about twice as large as the flashlight lens. What size is the shadow now? Finally, repeat the experiment with a disk that is the same size as the flashlight lens. What size is the shadow now? What rule can you deduce about the size of a shadow.

Q How does the length of your shadow vary during the day? Why does this happen?

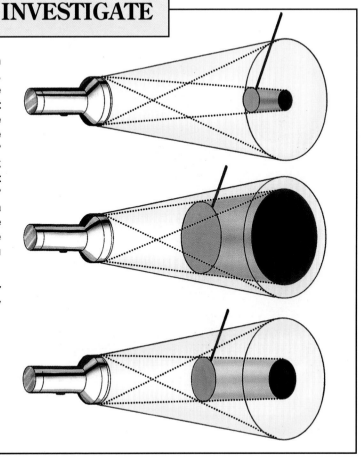

Seeing light

Your eye is basically a light-tight ball with a hole at the front and a light-sensitive layer at the back. Like a camera, your eye uses a lens to focus an image (picture) onto the light-sensitive layer.

Inside the eye

The front of the eye is covered by a transparent layer called the cornea. The colored part of the eye is a muscle called the iris. In the middle of the iris is a black area called the pupil. This is the hole that lets light into the eye. The iris automatically makes the pupil larger or smaller to let in more or less light, depending upon the lighting conditions.

The human eye. The retina contains about 137 million light-sensitive cells in an area the size of a small postage stamp. The optic nerve contains about 1 million nerve fibers. The focusing muscles of the eye adjust about 100,000 times a day. To exercise the leg muscles to the same extent would need a walk of 50 miles (80 km).

16

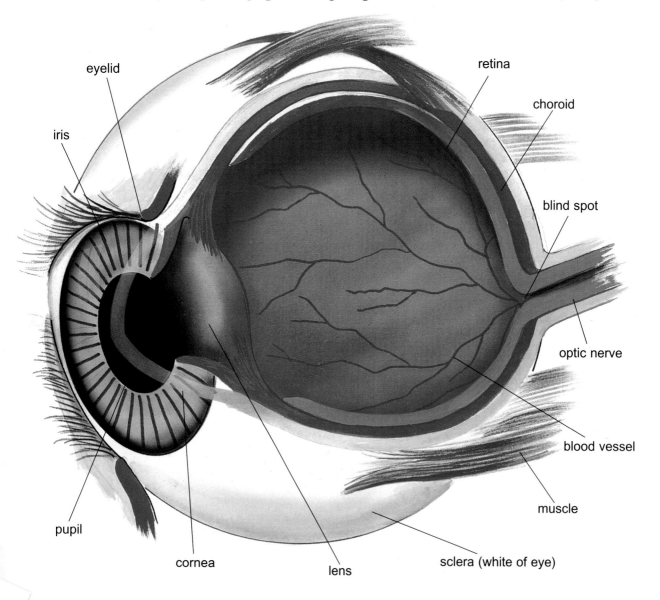

eyelid

iris

pupil

cornea

lens

retina

choroid

blind spot

optic nerve

blood vessel

muscle

sclera (white of eye)

Light entering the eye through the pupil passes through a lens which can alter its shape to focus images on the retina, the light-sensitive layer at the back of the eye. The human retina contains over 130 million light-sensitive cells called rods and cones. The rods are sensitive to black and white and shades of gray, and the cones are sensitive to color.

Blind spot

The rods and cones convert the light into electrical signals which are carried to the brain by the optic nerve. The point at which the optic nerve is attached to the retina is not sensitive to light; it is known as the blind spot. When an image is focused on the blind spot, nothing is seen.

Correcting eye defects

Some eye defects can be corrected by using another lens to aid the lens of the eye. The type of lens used in eyeglasses depends upon whether the person is near-sighted or far-sighted. In a near-sighted eye, the eye's lens focuses light in front of the retina. A concave lens helps focus light on the retina. A far-sighted eye focuses light behind the retina. A convex lens is used to correct the defect.

INVESTIGATE

Close your left eye and hold this page at arm's length. Look at the left dot with your right eye. You will see the right dot out of the corner of your eye. While you continue to look at the left dot, move the page very slowly toward you. Somewhere along the way, when the image of the dot is formed on the blind spot of your eye, the right dot will disappear. If you continue to move the page closer, the dot will reappear.

IT'S AMAZING!

The eyes of the toad are eight times more sensitive to light than our own.

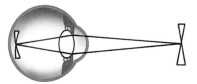

▲ When you look at a distant object, the lens of your eye is thin and the image is focused on the retina of the eye. When looking at a close object, the lens has to bulge to focus the image.

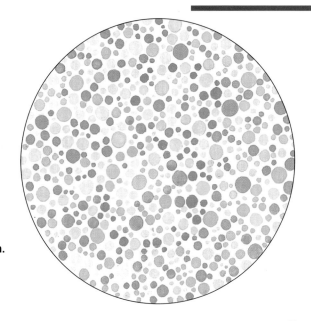

▶ About 8% of men 1% women are colorblind. They cannot tell the difference between red, green and gray. A colorblind person would not easily see the figure 8 in this diagram.

Polarized light

Try this experiment. Tie one end of a piece of thin rope to a door knob and hold the other end. Now move your hand up and down, producing a wave in the rope. This type of wave is called a vertical transverse wave because it vibrates in a vertical plane. Next, move your hand from side to side. You will produce another type of wave, known as a horizontal transverse wave because it vibrates in a horizontal plane.

If you move your hand in a diagonal direction, you produce a third type of wave, a combination of vertical and horizontal transverse waves. Light is like this. It is a combination of waves, each vibrating in a different plane. It contains a horizontal transverse wave, a vertical transverse wave, and many types of diagonal transverse waves

If we isolate or separate any of the waves in light, we have a special kind of light, called polarized light. Polarized light consists of waves which are vibrating in one direction only.

Producing polarized light

Now, in your experiment, leave the rope tied to the door knob, but pass the rope through a vertical slit, such as between the slats in the back of a chair. When you move your hand up and down, the wave produced will pass through the slit. However, what happens if you move your hand from side to side? You will create a horizontal transverse wave,

18

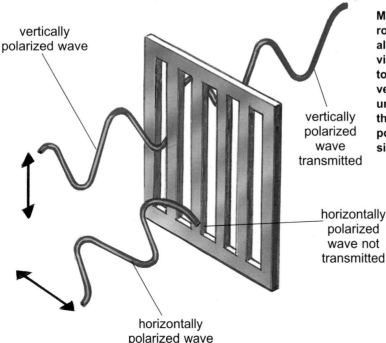

vertically
polarized wave

vertically
polarized
wave
transmitted

horizontally
polarized
wave not
transmitted

horizontally
polarized wave

Making polarized waves with a rope. The slats of a chair back allow only waves which are vibrating in the vertical direction to pass through. The result is a vertically polarized wave. When unpolarized light passes through a polarizing plate, polarized light is produced in a similar way.

but the wave will stop when it reaches the slit. The slit will only let vertical transverse waves pass through it.

A similar thing can be done with light waves by using special materials or lenses. These materials consist of millions of small crystals shaped like needles. The crystals permit only light waves that vibrate in a particular direction to pass through the material. The material used is known as a polarized plate or lens. When ordinary unpolarized light is shone through a polarizing plate, polarized light emerges.

Polarizing sunglasses absorb light which is vibrating horizontally (horizontally polarized). By absorbing the horizontally polarized light. sunglasses reduce glare. The light reflected from water is horizontally polarized so polarizing sunglasses are especially useful at the seaside.

IT'S AMAZING!

Over 1,000 years ago, the Vikings used polarized light to navigate over the seas. They carried a seemingly magical crystal, called a sunstone. This crystal let polarized light through only when it was held at a certain angle. The Vikings used the sunstone to locate a band of polarized light around the sun, even on cloudy days, and this helped them find their way.

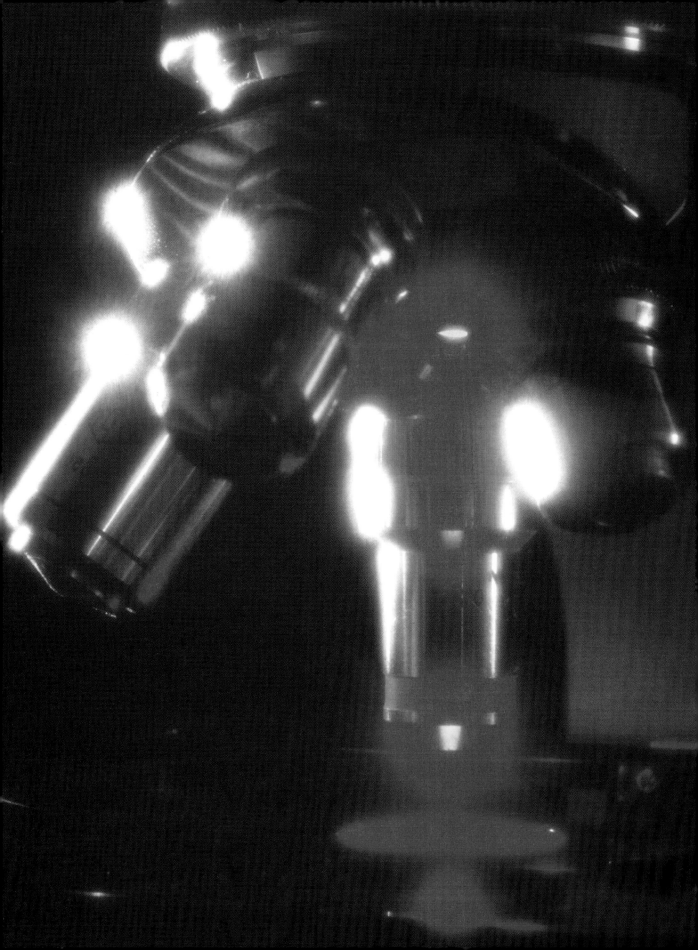

2
Using light

Sight is the most important of our senses, and our eyes are amazingly acute. Looking up at the night sky, you can see objects – stars – that are billions of miles (or kilometers) away. Even so, the unaided eye has its limits.

The eye's power can be increased by using optical instruments, such as the telescope and the microscope. The telescope lets us see faint stars and distant objects clearly. The microscope lets us see small objects. Another instrument that uses light is the laser, found in many unexpected places: the supermarket checkout, the operating room, and the home stereo system, for example.

In order to design and build these instruments, scientists need to understand how light behaves when it bounces off mirrors, and when it passes through transparent materials, such as lenses. Lenses are the key to most optical instruments but mirrors can also be used as well.

Optical instruments increase the power of our eyes. An ordinary microscope (left) magnifies around 2,000 times, allowing us to see objects one hundred times smaller than the finest details visible to our unaided eye. (right) At night, a sharp-eyed person can see around 2,500 stars in the sky. However, with binoculars or a small telescope, many thousands more can be seen.

Bouncing light

When light strikes a polished surface, it bounces off in much the same way that a ball thrown against a wall bounces off the wall. This process is called reflection of light.

Law of reflection

When a light beam is reflected off a mirror, it is possible to calculate the angle at which the beam will "bounce off" the mirror. The light beam that strikes the mirror is known as the incident ray. The angle between the incident ray and a perpendicular drawn to the mirror surface is know as the angle of incidence. The light ray that has bounced off the mirror is called the reflected ray, and the angle between this ray and the perpendicular is known as the angle of reflection. In every case, the angle of incidence is equal to the angle of reflection. This is called the "Law of Reflection."

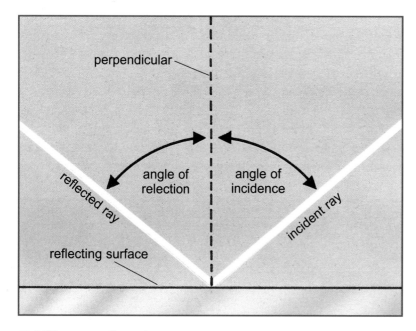

The law of reflection: the angle of incidence equals the angle of reflection.

Diffuse reflection

The law of reflection is true under all conditions, whether the reflecting surface is smooth or rough. However, when a beam of light strikes a rough surface, the reflected light is spread out. The light is sent in all directions by the rough surface. This is called diffuse reflection. When a beam of light strikes a smooth surface, such as a mirror, the reflected beam is not spread out. This is called regular reflection.

Images in mirrors

You see an image in a mirror because the reflected light seems to be coming from behind the mirror. If you look at an image of yourself in a mirror, you will notice that the image is behind the mirror at the same distance as you are in front of it. Now, close your right eye. You will see that it appears in the mirror as though you have closed your left eye. It appears that, in the mirror, left has become right and right has become left.

23

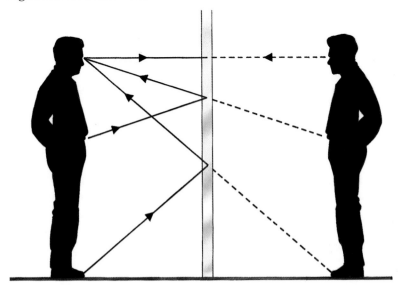

Q Why is the image of the far shore reflected in a lake upside down?

A single reflection causes a clock to be seen reversed left-to-right. Using two mirrors, placed at an angle to each other, the clock can be seen the correct way round.

INVESTIGATE

Produce reversed writing by placing a piece of carbon paper, carbon side up, under a sheet of plain paper. Write something on the paper. Look at the other side of the paper and you will see reversed writing. In what way is the writing reversed? Read the writing by holding it in front of a mirror. How does the paper have to be positioned? Why does the mirror let you read the writing? Write something on the paper while you look in the mirror. Can you produce reversed writing in this way?

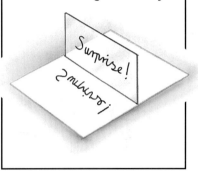

Curved mirrors

A mirror can be curved. At a fairground, curved mirrors are used in the "Hall of Mirrors" to produce amusing images. In the curved mirrors, you may appear to have a long thin body, or a flattened head.

Concave and convex mirrors

A spoon acts as a curved mirror. If you look into a polished spoon, it acts as a curved mirror. You will see an upside down image in the bowl of the spoon. A mirror that curves inward like the bowl of a spoon is called a concave mirror.

If you turn the spoon over, the surface will form a mirror that bulges outward. This is called a convex mirror. Your image will no longer be upside down. You might notice that you can see almost all of the room around you; a convex mirror produces a wide-angle image.

The focus

Parallel light rays falling on a concave mirror are reflected so that they converge (come together) at a fixed point,

IT'S AMAZING!

The largest single mirror telescope is on Mount Semirodriki, in the Caucasus Mountains of Russia. Its mirror weighs 77 tons (70 tonnes) and is 236 inches (6 m) cross. The telescope is so sensitive that it can detect a candle 15,000 miles (24,000 km) away. The next largest telescope is the Hale telescope at Mount Palomar, near Pasadena, California. This has a mirror 200 inches (508 cm) across which weighs 22 tons (20 tonnes).

INVESTIGATE

Obtain a concave mirror, such as a shaving mirror. Attach a piece of carbon paper to cardboard. Using the mirror, focus the sun's rays on the paper. What happens? Now, hold the mirror so that light from a window falls on it. Hold the cardboard in front of the mirror. What do you see? Is the image upright?

called the focus of the mirror. The distance between the focus and the mirror is called the focal length of the mirror. With a convex mirror, the rays diverge or spread out instead; they do not come to a focus.

Using curved mirrors

A shaving mirror is a concave mirror with a short focal length. The mirror produces a magnified upright image of a nearby object. A more distant object can be seen as a small upside down image on a piece of paper held near the focus. Concave mirrors are used in car headlights to produce a parallel beam of light. They are also used to collect light in reflecting telescopes.

Convex mirrors are used where a wide-angle view is needed. The side view mirrors in a car are convex mirrors, because the driver needs to see a wide area of the road behind the car. Convex mirrors are also used to watch for shoplifters in supermarkets.

Inside an astronomical telescope. A large curved mirror collects light from the stars and focuses it at the observation platform. The image is then photographed or stored on computer.

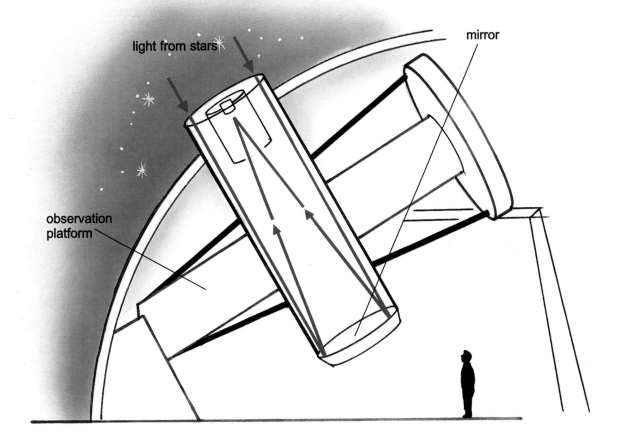

light from stars

mirror

observation platform

IT'S AMAZING!

In ordinary glass, light slows down to 124,000 miles/second (200,000 km/second). In diamond, it slows to 77,000 miles/second (124,000 km/second) while, in the exotic gem rutile, light barely reaches a speed of 62,000 miles/second (100,000 km/second).

Bending light

Light rays bend and change direction when they pass from one transparent material to another. This bending is called refraction. Refraction explains why a pencil in a jar of water appears bent or broken.

Slowing down

Refraction occurs because light travels at different speeds in different materials. For example, light travels more slowly in glass than in air. When a truck runs onto boggy ground where it travels more slowly, its wheels slow down on one side. This changes the direction of the truck. Light is refracted in the same way when it enters a material, such as glass, in which it slows.

Refractive index

A number, called the refractive index, tells us how slowly light will travel through a material. The refractive index of

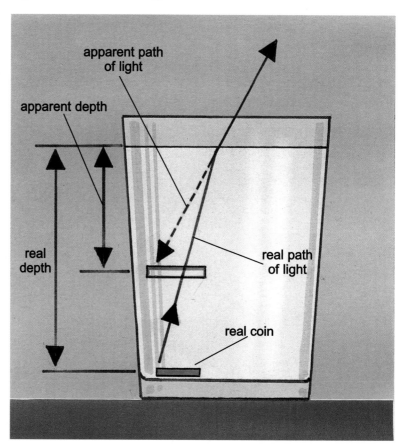

A coin in a glass of water appears much nearer the surface than it really is. This happens because light from the coin bends as it leaves the water. Our eyes misjudge where the coin actually is. The real depth divided by apparent depth gives the refractive index of water.

INVESTIGATE

Dissolve as much sugar as possible in a cup of hot water. Add a little coffee. Now fill a glass jar with cold water. Using a spoon, pour a few drops of the sugar solution into the cold water. What do you see? Why does this happen?

a material equals the speed of light in empty space divided by the speed of light in the material. The refractive index of water is 1.3; this means that light slows down to 143,000 miles/second in water.

Shallow pools

When light bends, it may trick us into seeing things in the wrong place. A river may look shallower than it actually is. Light from the bottom of the river bends as it leaves the water, making the bottom of the river appear closer than it really is. For the same reason, a coin in a glass of water appears much nearer to the surface than it really is.

Mirages

Mirages occur when light from the sky is bent upwards by a hot air layer near the ground. The light appears to come from the ground; it looks like a pool of blue water on the ground. This is called a mirage. Mirages have fooled many travelers in the desert into thinking that there was a lake or ocean just ahead. Sometimes, a hot layer of air can occur above the ground. Light from a distant object can then be refracted downwards by the hot air, causing the object to appear much closer than it really is.

▼**When light bends, we can see things in the wrong place. A mirage occurs when light from a distant object is bent by a layer of warm air near the ground. As a result, we see the object near the ground.**

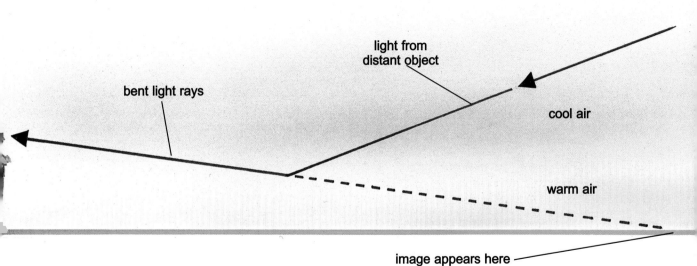

light from distant object

bent light rays

cool air

warm air

image appears here

Lenses

A lens is a piece of transparent material with at least one side curved. There are two main kinds of lenses: convex and concave. Convex lenses have surfaces that bulge outward at the center. Concave lenses have surfaces that bulge inward at the center.

Getting into focus

When a beam of light passes through a convex lens, it converges or comes closer together. If the beam comes from a very distant object, it converges to a single point called the focus. When a beam of light passes through a concave lens, the beam diverges or spreads out. Parallel light rays spread out as if they were coming from a single point, called the focus. In both cases, the distance between the focus and the middle of the lens is called the focal length.

28

INVESTIGATE

Fill a clear glass jar with water and screw the top on tightly. Shine a flashlight through the jar. Can you bring the light to a focus? Can you find the focal length of the jar? Look at an object through the jar. The shape of the object seen through the jar depends upon whether the jar is upright or on its side. How can you produce an enlarged image with the jar?

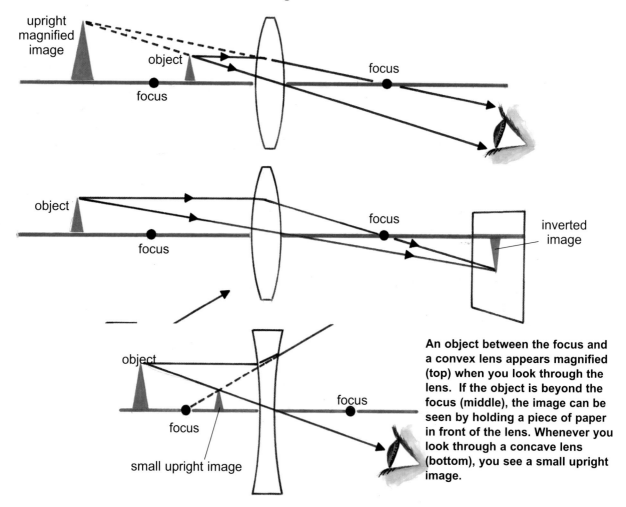

upright magnified image

object

focus

focus

focus

object

focus

focus

inverted image

object

focus

focus

small upright image

An object between the focus and a convex lens appears magnified (top) when you look through the lens. If the object is beyond the focus (middle), the image can be seen by holding a piece of paper in front of the lens. Whenever you look through a concave lens (bottom), you see a small upright image.

Forming images

A convex lens makes a good magnifying glass. If you place a small object between the focus and the lens, and look at the object through the lens, you will see a magnified image of the object. The magnifying power depends on the focal length of the lens. The thicker the lens, the shorter the focal length and the more it magnifies.

If you place a bright object further away from the lens than the focus, you will not see an image through the lens. But if you hold a piece of paper on the opposite side of the lens from the object, you should be able to see an upside down image of the object on the paper.

For a concave lens, the image is always on the same side of the lens as the object. It is always smaller than the object and cannot be focused onto paper.

Above right: The lenses used in lighthouses are made from a series of glass rings. They are called Fresnel lenses after French physicist Augustin Fresnel (1788-1827). These lenses cannot produce clear images but they concentrate light into strong beams.

Right: The magnification of a lens is the number of times the image seen is larger than the oject viewed. The thicker the lens the greater the magnification produced. However, very fat lenses distort the image so that it cannot be seen clearly.

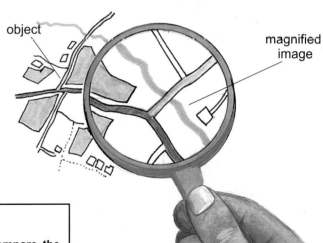

object

magnified image

INVESTIGATE

Focus a magnifying glass over some lined paper. Compare the number of lines seen outside the lens with a single line seen through the lens. What is the magnifying power of the lens? Repeat the experiment with other convex lenses. Do fat lenses magnify more than thin lenses? Does the width of the lens have any effect on the image?

▶ A slide projector uses a convex lens to produce a magnified image of a slide. The image is real and can projected onto a screen

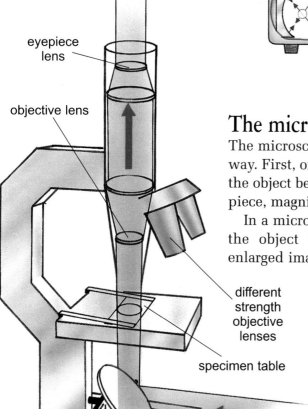

eyepiece lens

objective lens

different strength objective lenses

specimen table

mirror reflects light on to specimen above

Optical instruments

The magnifying glass is a simple optical instrument. It uses a lens to produce an enlarged image. Another simple optical instrument is the movie projector. This projects an image on a screen.

Real and virtual images

An image that can be focused on a screen or piece of paper is called a real image. This is the kind of image produced by a movie projector. An image that cannot be focused on a screen is called a virtual image. The magnified image seen through a convex lens or magnifying glass is virtual.

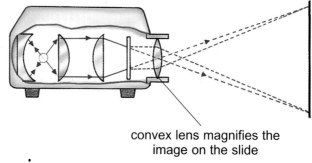

convex lens magnifies the image on the slide

The microscope

The microscope and telescope both use lenses in a similar way. First, one lens, called the objective, forms an image of the object being viewed. Then another lens, called the eyepiece, magnifies the image.

In a microscope, the objective is the lower lens, close to the object being viewed. The objective produces an enlarged image of the object. This image is then magnified

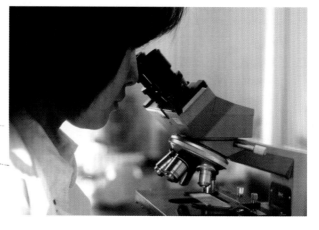

by the upper lens, or eyepiece. The lenses are mounted at the ends of two tubes. One tube slides inside the other so that the image can be focused.

The telescope

A telescope that uses lenses is called a refracting telescope, or refractor. The objective of a refractor is a large lens at the front. The eyepiece is a smaller lens at the rear. The telescope is focused by moving the eyepiece backward and forward until a clear image is seen.

Some telescopes have a convex lens objective and a concave lens as an eyepiece. This produces an upright image. Astronomer's telescopes have convex lenses for both objective and eyepiece. This produces an upside down image – this does not matter since stars are points of light.

Binoculars

Binoculars consist of a pair of telescopes side by side. Light entering the front lens travels through a pair of prisms. The prisms turn the image right side up. They also mean that the binoculars do not have to be very long.

31

INVESTIGATE

Darken all the windows in a room except one. Ask a friend to hold a convex lens (a magnifying glass, for example) by the window directed at the scene outside. Bring a piece of white paper slowly near the lens until a focused image is formed. What do you notice about the image? What optical instrument is similar to your arrangement?

▼ **Inside binoculars, the light rays are bent around by a pair of prisms. This means that the binoculars do not have to be very long. The prisms also turn the image right-way up.**

◄◄ **A modern microscope usually has several objective lenses of different strength which can be swung into place when required. The binocular microscope has two eyepieces and is easier to use for long periods.**

Lasers

A laser is a device that produces a narrow, powerful beam of brightly colored light. Lasers have many uses. A laser beam can be used to cut through steel or to drill tiny holes in hard materials such as diamond. Doctors use lasers to perform delicate eye and brain operations. Dentists use lasers to remove decay from teeth. Low-power lasers are used at supermarket checkouts to read barcodes and in compact disc players. Lasers are also used to make three-dimensional photographs called holograms.

What L-A-S-E-R really means

The word laser is really a set of initials that stands for Light Amplification by Stimulated Emission of Radiation. This name was chosen because a laser persuades, or stimulates, its atoms to amplify a flash of light.

How a laser works

Inside a laser, light energy from a powerful flash tube is absorbed by the atoms of the laser material. The atoms can only hold this extra energy for a short time. When they release the energy again, it is in the form of light particles, or photons, which stimulate more atoms to release light. More light is produced and the process is repeated until an intense beam of light builds up. The beam is reflected back

32

IT'S AMAZING!

How far to the moon?

A laser beam was reflected off the moon for the first time on May 9, 1962, using a telescope at the Massachusetts Institute of Technology, Cambridge, Massachusetts. The beam covered an area 4 miles (6.4 km) wide on the moon. By measuring the time taken for the beam to travel to the moon and return, the distance to the moon was found.

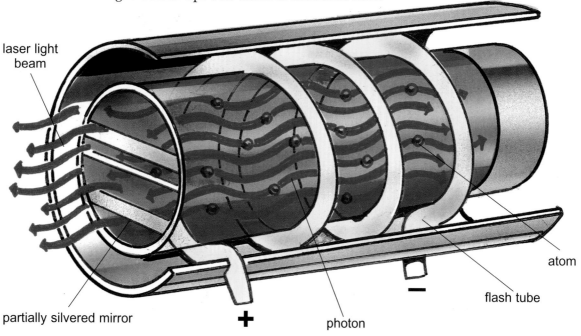

laser light beam

partially silvered mirror

+

photon

atom

flash tube

−

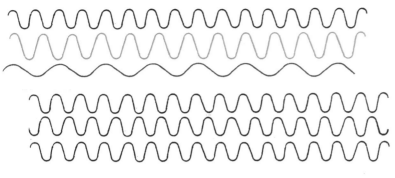

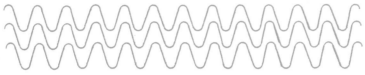

White light (top) is a mixture of different wavelengths. In light of a single color (middle), all the waves have the same wavelength but are out of step. In laser light (bottom), all the waves have the same wavelength and are in step.

and forth between mirrors at the ends of the laser. Eventually the beam becomes so powerful that it bursts out one end of the laser as an intense beam of light.

A laser cutting metal.

Laser light

Laser light is different from ordinary light. In ordinary light, the waves are all out of step with each other. Also, ordinary white light is a mixture of colors, with each color having a different wavelength. In laser light, all the waves have exactly the same wavelength, so laser light is one pure color. Also, in laser light, all the waves are exactly in step. The peaks and valleys of the waves line up with each other.

▶ **A laser cutting metal.**

3
Light and color

There are many fascinating puzzles about light and color. What causes colors? Why do objects have different colors in different lights? Why are new colors produced when paints are mixed? To answer these questions, we must look at how color is produced and how light is absorbed or reflected by objects.

An important discovery about light and color was made by Isaac Newton. He discovered that white light, for example sunlight, was really a mixture of colors. This can be demonstrated by a simple experiment with a prism. In nature, the colors are revealed when sunlight passes through a raindrop and forms a rainbow.

Each color of the rainbow corresponds to a different wavelength in the spectrum of electromagnetic waves. Objects owe their color to the fact that they absorb some wavelengths from white light and reflect others. The way colored lights and paints mix can be explained in the same way.

◀ A rainbow shows that white light is made up of a combination of colors. The colors are separated when the light passes through raindrops.

▶ A sunset is red because the sky absorbs the blue part of sunlight and only the red part reaches your eyes.

Colors

In 1665, Isaac Newton, performed an important experiment. He passed a narrow beam of sunlight, or "white light," through a triangular glass prism. He found that the white light split into a multicolored beam, consisting of violet, indigo, blue, green, yellow, orange, and red. This band of colors is known as the color spectrum.

Newton also found that he could pass the color spectrum through another upside down prism and produce white light. In other words, he could recombine the colors of the spectrum to produce white light. Clearly, white light is a combination of all the colors of the spectrum.

Spectrum in the sky

The rainbow is nature's color spectrum. It can be seen only when you are facing away from the sun. Furthermore, the sky behind the rainbow must be hazy or cloudy. It is the clouds or haze that make the rainbow possible.

Remember the colors of the spectrum by thinking about Mr. Biv. His full name is Roy G. Biv (which stands for red, orange, yellow, green, blue, indigo, violet).

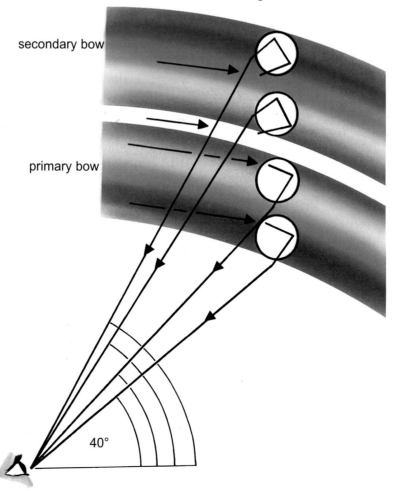

secondary bow

primary bow

40°

A rainbow is seen when light rays from the Sun are reflected by raindrops, which act as tiny prisms. Sometimes a second bow is seen outside the brighter primary bow. The colors of the secondary bow are reversed, with red on the inside of the bow. This is caused by light being reflected twice inside the raindrops; the primary bow is caused when light is reflected once within the raindrop.

The haze or clouds consist of millions of drops of water, and each drop acts as a prism breaking sunlight into a spectrum. Each drop reflects only a single color directly into our eyes, the color depending upon the height of the drop above the horizon.

Sometimes a weaker rainbow (called the secondary bow) is seen outside the bright main bow. This occurs when light is reflected twice within the raindrops before emerging. The additional reflection has the effect of reversing the order of the colors. Red appears at the inner edge of the secondary bow, while it appears at the outside of the main bow.

Wavelength and color

The light that we can see (called visible light) consists of electromagnetic waves. Each color corresponds to a different wavelength in the spectrum. Orange light has a wavelength of around 600 thousand millionths of a meter, or 600 nanometers. Green light has a wavelength of around 500 nanometers, and violet around 400 nanometers.

Q Estimate the wavelength of yellow light. Yellow lies between green and orange in the spectrum.

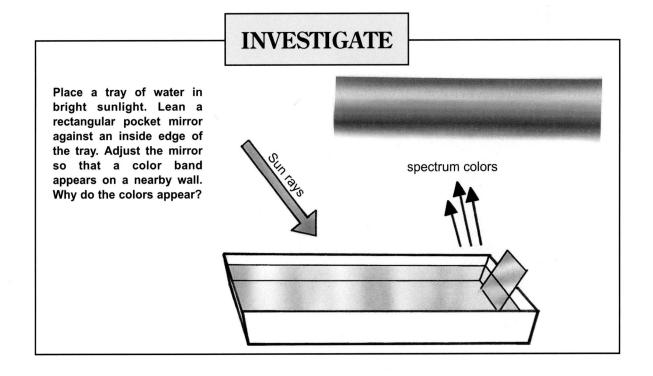

INVESTIGATE

Place a tray of water in bright sunlight. Lean a rectangular pocket mirror against an inside edge of the tray. Adjust the mirror so that a color band appears on a nearby wall. Why do the colors appear?

Sun rays

spectrum colors

Colored objects

An opaque object reflects certain colors and absorbs other colors. The color of an object depends upon the color of the light it reflects. A red object appears red because it reflects red light and absorbs other colors. A green object appears green because it reflects green light and absorbs other colors.

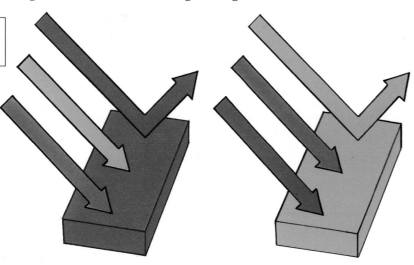

Black and white

According to scientists, neither white nor black are really colors. A white object reflects all colors. If you view a white object in red light, it appears red because it reflects red light. If it is viewed in green light, it appears green because it reflects green light. A black object reflects no light. It appears black whatever color light shines on it.

If an object only reflects red light, it appears red. The other colors are absorbed. If it reflects only green light, it appears green. If it reflects only blue light, it appears blue.

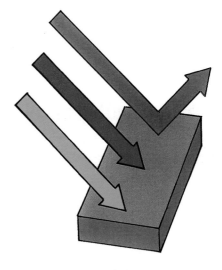

When light falls on a blackboard every color in the light is absorbed. This makes the board appear black. The white chalk, however, reflects every color. This is why the chalk appears white.

Black apples

If no light is reflected from an object, the object appears black. At night, everything looks black because there is no light to be reflected from the objects around you. If you look at a red apple under a blue light bulb, the apple appears to be black since there is no red light to be reflected by the apple.

More than one color

An object can reflect more than one color. This happens because the dyes or paints used to color many objects are not pure colors. For example, yellow paint often contains some green pigment. So a yellow painted wall will reflect some green light as well as yellow light. In white light, we see a yellow-green wall. If the light waves falling on the wall are yellow, we see a yellow wall. If green light falls on the wall, we see a green wall.

Colored glass

Translucent objects, such as colored glass, allow some colors to pass through them and block other colors. We see the color that passes through the glass. Red glass, for example, lets red light pass through and absorbs other colors.

Q What color would a blue book look in green light? in red light? in blue light? in white light?

A chameleon can change the color of its skin by changing the arrangement of colored granules in its skin. The color changes are caused by varying temperature or lighting conditions. The colors also change if the chameleon is excited. In the early morning, some chamleons become black to help them absorb the heat of the Sun.

Mixing colors

You may have noticed that the picture on a television screen is made up of tiny stripes or dots of only three colors: red, green, and blue. All the colors on the screen are produced by combining various amounts of these three colors. Red, green, and blue are called primary colors because they can be mixed to make any color. White light is produced by mixing equal amounts of red, green, and blue light.

Some pairs of colored lights add together to make white light. They are called complementary colors. Yellow and blue are complementary colors, for example.

Mixing paints

Mixing colored paints involves a different color production process from mixing colored lights. You probably know that mixing blue and yellow paints makes green. This happens because the pigments in the paints are not pure colors. Blue paint contains pigment that reflects blue light, which is why the paint appears blue. But it also contains some green and indigo pigments, too. In the same way, yellow paint reflects a little red and green as well as yellow. A mixture of the paints appears green because green is the only color reflected by both paints.

When mixing paints (left), any color can be made by mixing red, blue and yellow. These three colors are the primary colors when mixing paints. The secondary colors (made by mixing two colors) are orange, green and purple. When mixing lights (right), the primary colors are red, green and blue. The secondary colors are magenta (bluish red), cyan (bluish green) and yellow. Any color can be produced by mixing the correct proportion of red, green and blue light. When all three are mixed, the result is white light.

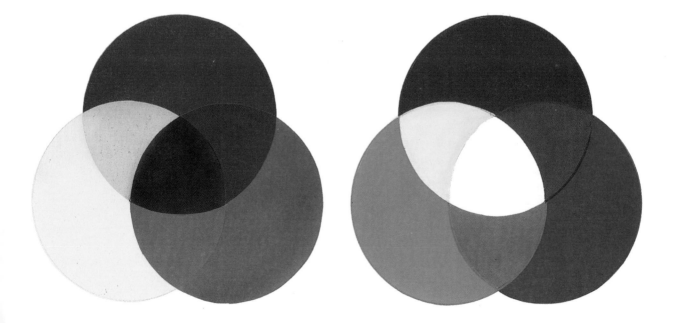

With paints, the primary colors are blue, yellow, and red. Any color paint can be produced by mixing paints of these colors. If blue, yellow, and red are mixed, you get black or a dark grayish brown.

Why is the sky blue?

The air around the Earth is composed of many tiny particles, including dust and water vapor. During the day, as sunlight passes through the air, the blue light waves are reflected by the particles while the other waves are unaffected. The blue waves are reflected into our eyes and the sky appears blue. At sunset, when the sun is low down on the horizon, the blue light is reflected away from our eyes. We see the light that remains, and the sky appears red.

Light from the Sun is reflected by dust particles in the atmosphere. Blue light is scattered more strongly than red light. This makes the sky away from the Sun appear blue during the day. When we look toward the setting Sun, we see the unscattered red light.

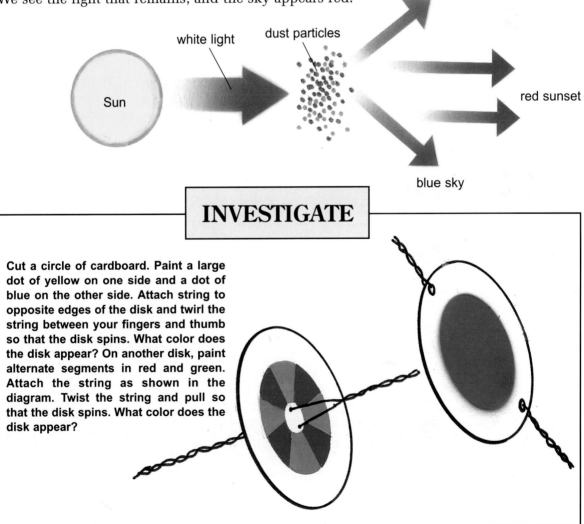

blue sky

white light · dust particles

Sun

red sunset

blue sky

INVESTIGATE

Cut a circle of cardboard. Paint a large dot of yellow on one side and a dot of blue on the other side. Attach string to opposite edges of the disk and twirl the string between your fingers and thumb so that the disk spins. What color does the disk appear? On another disk, paint alternate segments in red and green. Attach the string as shown in the diagram. Twist the string and pull so that the disk spins. What color does the disk appear?

4

Talking, music, and noise

Humans have always communicated by using sound. The first attempts to communicate were probably through grunts and gestures. When languages developed, complex ideas could be expressed and human civilization began. Words, and music, became an important part of human life.

Sounds are produced by vibrations. Place your fingers at the side of your throat and you will feel the vibrations produced as you speak. The vibrations produce waves in the air - these are sound waves. We hear the sounds when the waves enter our ears.

Speech and musical sounds are different from noise; their waves are produced by regular vibrations, and musical sounds have a definite frequency or pitch. Noise, on the other hand, is a random mixture of many frequencies. We need to eliminate noise if we are to understand the message being carried by sound waves. In particular, noise needs to be eliminated from recordings of music if we are to enjoy them.

Q Name as many different sounds as possible, such as crash (dish falling and breaking), thud (falling weight), clang (hitting an anvil with hammer). What makes the following sounds: clatter, crackle, tick, crunch, bang, patter, tinkle, rumble?

◄ **The sound of marching band adds to the excitement of a parade. The sounds carry to the listening crowd as waves in the air. The sounds can be musical or noisy, loud or soft depending on the properties of the waves.**

Making and hearing sounds

Sound and light are similar in some ways. Both travel as waves and both can be reflected and refracted. However, they are produced in different ways, they travel in different ways, and we detect them in different ways.

Making sounds

Sounds are made when objects vibrate, or move rapidly to and fro. If you pluck the string of a guitar, you will see the string vibrate and hear the sound produced.

When an object vibrates, it pushes air molecules in front of it, compressing them. This creates a small area of high pressure where the molecules are crowded together. As the vibrating object moves back in the opposite direction, the air molecules can spread out slightly. This creates an area of low pressure. In this way, the object creates areas of high and low pressure as it vibrates. The areas of high and low pressure move outward from the object as waves in the air – sound waves.

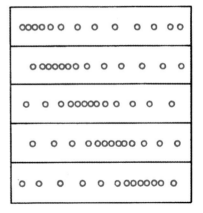

▲ Sound waves disturb the molecules as they pass through the air. The molecules bunch together to form an area of high pressure which travels outward from the source of the sound.

▼ A tuning fork vibrates when it is struck The vibrations produce sound waves in the air.

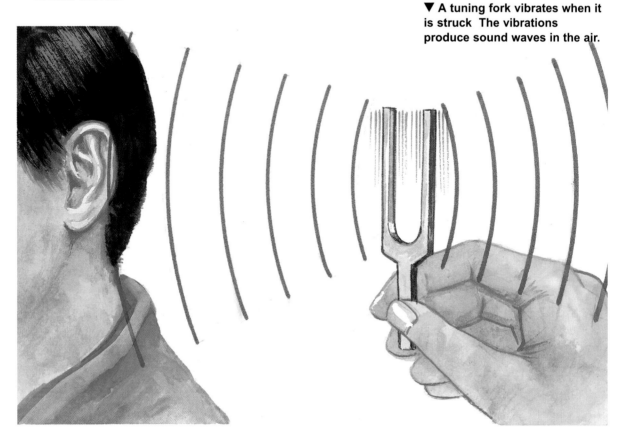

No sound in space

If there is no air surrounding a vibrating object, no sound waves can be produced. Sound waves can only exist in a material whose molecules can move closer together and farther apart. This means that sound waves can travel through liquids, solids, and gases, but not through empty space. This is one difference between light and sound waves – light waves can travel through empty space but sound waves cannot.

Hearing sounds

We hear a sound when sound waves enter our ears. The outer flap of the ear is a funnel that collects the waves and passes them along a short tube to the ear drum. The sound makes the drum vibrate, causing the tiny bones in contact with it to vibrate. These bones carry the sound to the inner ear. Here the vibrations are converted into electrical signals by a shell-shaped organ called the cochlea. The electrical signals are carried by nerves to the brain.

45

INVESTIGATE

Blow up a balloon. The balloon will contain a mixture of carbon dioxide and air. Hold the balloon between your ear and a watch. You will hear the sound of ticking more clearly than without the balloon. This is because sound waves travel more slowly through carbon dioxide than through air. The balloon acts like a converging lens and focuses the sound waves on your ear.

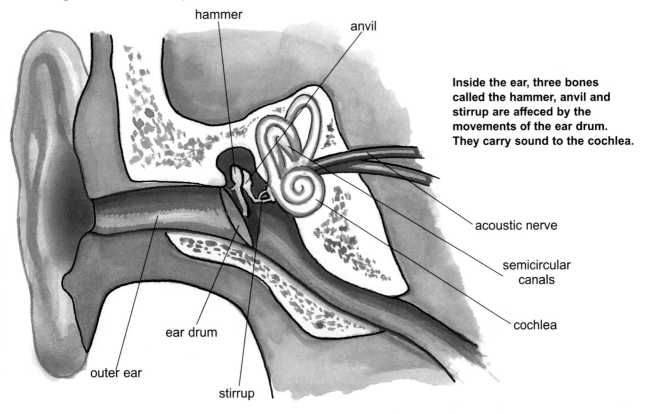

hammer

anvil

Inside the ear, three bones called the hammer, anvil and stirrup are affeced by the movements of the ear drum. They carry sound to the cochlea.

acoustic nerve

semicircular canals

cochlea

ear drum

outer ear

stirrup

▼ The frequency of a sound is measured in hertz (Hz). One hertz equals one wave per second. The diagram shows the frequency range that can be heard by humans and other animals.

Measuring sound

All sounds are different. Some are loud and some are soft. Some are high-pitched whistles and some are low-pitched rumbles. Some are pleasant and musical to listen to and some are unpleasant. What makes sounds so different? The answer is that sounds have different shaped waves and that most sounds are combinations of different waves.

Frequency and pitch

The distance between two successive peaks of a sound wave is called the wavelength of the sound. The wavelength of a wave is closely connected to its frequency, or the number of wave crests that pass a given point in one second. The greater the frequency, the higher the pitch of the sound we hear.

A wave with a long wavelength has a low frequency, and a wave with a short wavelength has a high frequency. High frequency, short wavelength waves make high-pitched sounds. Low-frequency, long wavelength waves make low-pitched sounds.

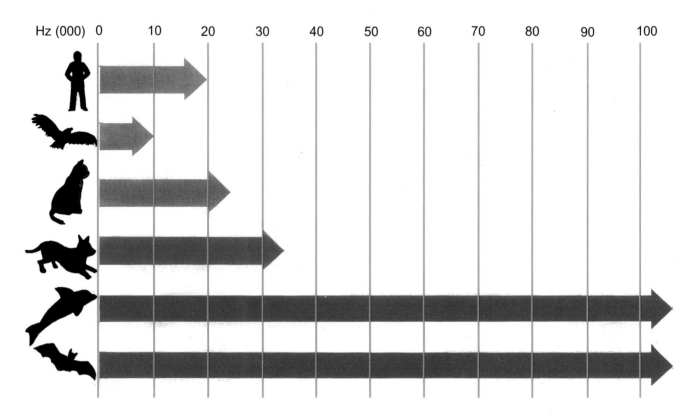

Hz (000) 0   10   20   30   40   50   60   70   80   90   100

IT'S AMAZING!

The call of the hump-back whale is the loudest noise made by a living creature. It is louder than Concorde supersonic airliner taking off, and can be detected up to 500 miles (800 km) away.

▼ **The loudness of sounds is measured in decibels (dB). The softest sound we can hear is rated around 0 dB. A jet aircraft taking off can produce a noise rated as 120 dB.**

Amplitude and loudness

The size of a vibration or wave is called the amplitude. The greater the amplitude, the louder the sound. When a guitar string is plucked strongly, the string moves a greater distance as it vibrates back and forth than if it were struck lightly. This means that a louder sound is produced.

The speed of sound

The speed at which sound waves travel depends upon the material they are traveling through. They travel faster in a denser medium, such as glass or water, than in air. For instance, sound waves travel at about 1,128 feet (344 m) per second in air, at about 4,792 feet (1,461 m) per second in water, and in steel at 16,400 feet (5,000 m) per second. The higher the temperature, the faster sound travels. So, the speed of sound is greater in hot weather than in cold weather.

Q Why does a mosquito make a high-pitched sound as it flies around the room?

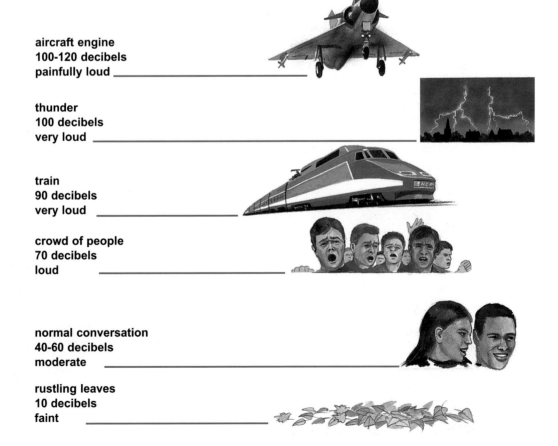

**aircraft engine
100-120 decibels
painfully loud**

**thunder
100 decibels
very loud**

**train
90 decibels
very loud**

**crowd of people
70 decibels
loud**

**normal conversation
40-60 decibels
moderate**

**rustling leaves
10 decibels
faint**

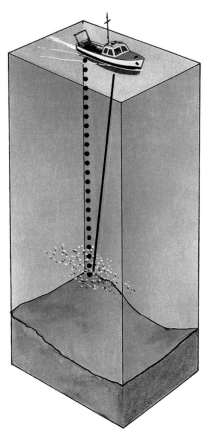

Bouncing sounds

Sound waves can be reflected; they can bounce off smooth, hard objects. An echo is a sound reflected off an object. Not all sounds are reflected. If they fall on a soft object, such as a cushion, they are absorbed and will not bounce off the object.

Using echoes

Echoes can be useful. Before radar was invented, sailors caught in fog sounded their fog horns. By listening to the echo, the sailors could tell if they were near dangerous cliffs or coastlines. Echoes are also used to locate underground oil deposits. When looking for oil, geologists set off underground explosions. The echoes from the explosions are detected and recorded by instruments called seismographs. Oil-bearing rocks produce a certain pattern of echoes. This allows the geologists to locate the oil.

In the concert hall

Acoustics is the study of sound in buildings, such as concert halls and theaters. In these buildings, it is important that sounds can be heard clearly.

▲ **Ships uses sonar (SOund Navigation And Ranging) to find the depth of the sea beneath them. The depth of the water is found by measuring the time for an echo to reflect off the sea bed.**

panels reflect the sound from the stage toward the audience

reflecting panels

▶ **In a concert hall, sound reflecting panels direct the sound of the orchestra toward the audience. Unwanted echos are reduced by sound-absorbing curtains and panels.**

One problem is that sound is reflected off the walls and ceilings, so that the audience hears a confusing mixture of echoes. The unwanted echoes are called reverberation. Reverberation can be reduced by padding the walls, hanging thick curtains, and padding seats.

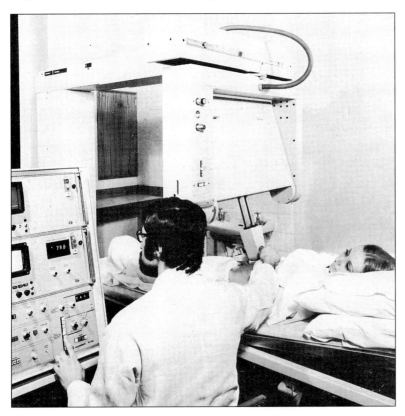

A pregnant woman receives an ultrasonic scan. The scanner transmits ultrasonic waves into her body and an image of the baby is displayed on a screen.

Silent sound

Humans cannot hear sounds with a frequency above 20,000 hertz. Sound with a higher frequency is called ultrasound. It is used in medicine to examine babies before they are born. A scanner transmits a beam of ultrasound into the mother's body. The beam is reflected by different parts of the baby's body. A scanner picks up the echoes and displays them as an image on a screen.

Whales, dolphins, and bats use ultrasound to navigate and locate their prey. They emit pulses of ultrasound, and the returning echoes show where obstacles or prey are. These echo-location systems are remarkably accurate. For example, the Rousettus fruit bat can locate objects only 0.02 inch (0.5 mm) across while flying at top speed.

INVESTIGATE

Tie one end of a fine steel wire (such as a guitar string) to a nail hammered into a thin piece of plywood. Attach a weight to the other end of the wire. Run the string over two clothespins as shown in the diagram. Do you get a musical note when the wire is plucked? Use a third clothespin to vary the length of the sounding wire. What effect does shortening the sounding wire have? Change the weight. What effect does a greater weight have?

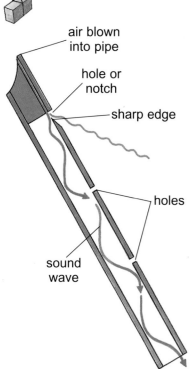

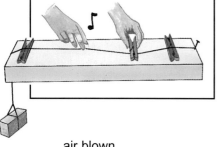

air blown into pipe

hole or notch

sharp edge

holes

sound wave

Musical sounds

Any sound that is pleasant to listen to is called musical. These sounds are produced by musical instruments such as the guitar, violin, trumpet, and drum. Musicians control the sounds that their instruments make, varying the pitch, loudness, and timing of the notes to produce a pleasant tune.

Musical instruments

There are four main types of musical instruments: strings, percussion, wind, and electronic instruments. A stringed instrument produces sound when a stretched string vibrates; the guitar and violin are stringed instruments. A percussion instrument produces sound when part of the instrument is struck; a drum is a percussion instrument. A wind instrument produces a sound when air is blown across a hole or past a reed; a flute is a wind instrument.

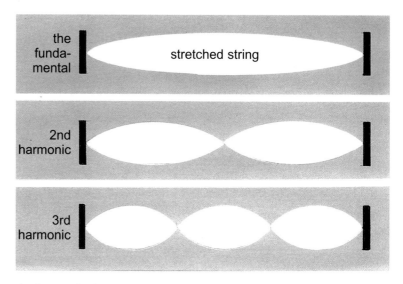

the fundamental — stretched string

2nd harmonic

3rd harmonic

▲ A stretched string can vibrate in different ways. If it vibrates from end to end (top), it produces its fundamental note. The string can also vibrate in two or three sections (middle and bottom), producing the second and third harmonic or overtone.

◀ A pipe contains a sharp edge against which air is blown. Sound waves are created in the air inside the pipe.

Pure notes

Each musical note has a definite frequency. For example, the note A has a frequency of 440 hertz, whether it is played on a guitar or a piano. However, no musical instrument produces a perfectly pure note. As well as the main note, called the fundamental, produced by an instrument, there are a number of fainter notes, called overtones. The overtones have two, three, four, five, and six times the frequency of the fundamental. Different instruments produce different mixtures of the fundamental and overtones. This is why different instruments sound different even if they are playing the same note.

51

Electronic instruments

Electronic sounds are produced by a loudspeaker rather than a musical instrument. The sounds are controlled by electrical signals produced by a keyboard, electric guitar, or computer. An electric guitar, for example, produces an electrical signal when its strings are plucked. These signals are fed to the loudspeaker and converted into sounds. Keyboards and synthesizers are able to store sounds as patterns of numbers. The numbers can be altered to change the pitch or frequency and other features of the sound — playing sounds backward, at different speeds, and with added echoes, for example.

▲ Rock bands use electric instruments because these instruments can amplify the sounds produced. These instruments can also produce many different musical effects.

Unpleasant sounds

Any sound that is unpleasant to hear is called noise. Very loud noises, such as sonic booms and fire engine sirens, can harm our ears.

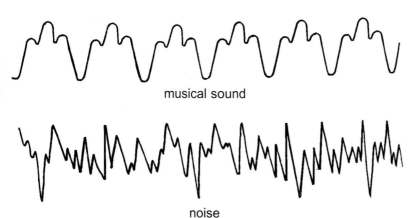

musical sound

noise

Sonic booms

A sonic boom is a noise produced by supersonic aircraft. As the aircraft flies slowly, sound waves spread out ahead of it. When the aircraft is traveling at the speed of sound, the waves cannot move ahead of the aircraft. A wall of compressed air, called a shock wave, forms in front of the plane. When the plane flies faster than the speed of sound, it leaves the shock wave behind. The trailing shock wave produces a tremendous noise, like a clap of thunder, as it passes over the ground; this is called the sonic boom.

▲ **Musical sounds have wave patterns which are evenly spaced and regular. Noise has an irregular and uneven wave pattern.**

▼ **When an aircraft exceeds the speed of sound (mach 1), a shock wave builds up at the nose of the craft, causing a sonic boom. The shock wave forms a cone behind the aircraft.**

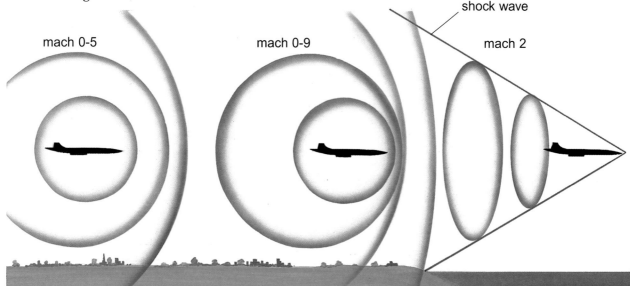

shock wave

mach 0-5   mach 0-9   mach 2

52

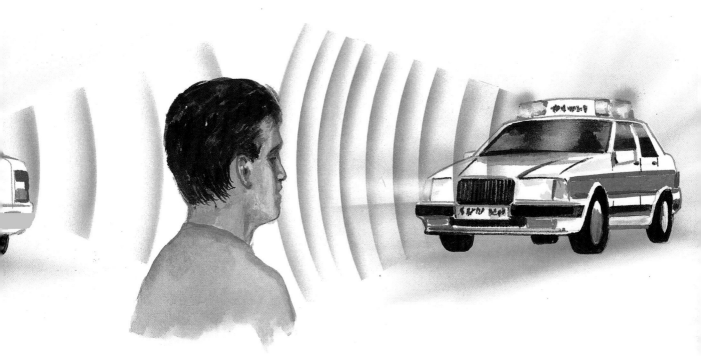

Changing sounds

The pitch of a fire engine's siren depends on whether the engine is traveling toward or away from you. When the engine is approaching, the sound waves ahead of it are crowded together by the movement of the engine. This increases the frequency of the waves and makes the siren sound high-pitched. When the engine is going away, the movement stretches out the waves behind it. This makes the waves have a lower frequency and the siren sounds low-pitched. This change of pitch of a moving sound is called the Doppler effect, after Austrian scientist Christian Johann Doppler who described it in 1842.

Anti-noise

It is possible to cancel out noise and produce quiet! This is done by measuring the pressure of the noise wave and mixing it with another wave that has the opposite pressure. The troughs of the original noise wave correspond to the peaks of the added wave. When the two sounds mix, they cancel each other out. This method is called "anti-noise." In hospitals, anti-noise is used to make body scanners quieter for the patient.

▲ **The Doppler effect. As a police car races away from you, sounding its siren, fewer sound waves reach you than when it approached you. This causes the siren's pitch to drop as the car passes you.**

IT'S AMAZING!

Light from distant galaxies changes color because the galaxies are moving. The light is redder than normal if the galaxies are moving away from the Earth. This is called the red shift; it is similar to the Doppler effect for sound.

Sound recording

There are two main ways of recording sound: analogue and digital. Analogue recordings store sound wave patterns as a groove cut in a record or as a magnetic pattern on plastic tape. Digital recordings store the sound wave patterns as a series of numbers (or digits) on a compact disc or digital audio tape.

54

Record player

On a record player, a stylus or needle rests in the groove of the record. As the record turns the needle vibrates against the bumps in the groove. The vibrations of the needle produce an electrical signal which varies in time with the recorded music or speech. The signal is fed to an amplifier. Here it is strengthened (amplified) before being sent to the speaker.

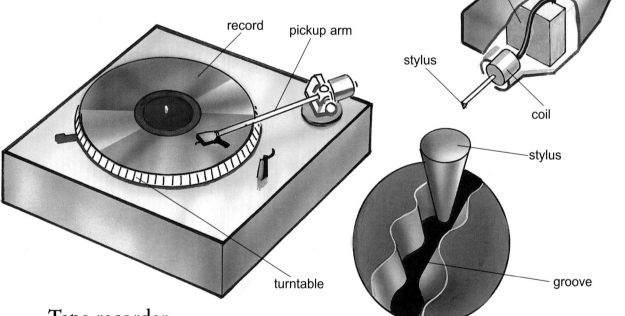

Tape recorder

The tape in a tape recorder is covered with a layer of magnetic particles. On an unrecorded tape, the particles of magnetic material point in random directions.

To make a tape recording, electrical signals from a microphone are fed to the recording head. This produces a magnetic force which arranges the particles on the tape into a pattern. To play back the recording, the tape is moved past a replay head. The magnetic pattern on the tape causes a signal in the replay head. The signal is then amplified and passed to the speaker.

A common kind of record player pickup contains a small magnet held near a wire coil. As the stylus bumps along the groove, it movements shake the magnet, producing an electric signal in the coil.

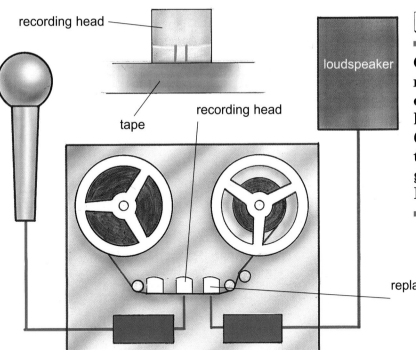

recording head

tape

recording head

loudspeaker

replay head

Compact disc

On a compact disc, the music is stored as a spiral of tiny holes or pits. The pits are the digits in the numbers which represent the recorded sound. The sounds are read by a laser beam shining on the disc from underneath. The laser beam is reflected off the disc if it does not shine on a hole in the disc. A system of mirrors and lenses directs the reflected beam to a light-sensitive device. This produces an electrical signal representing the recorded sound.

▲ When making a tape recording electrical signals in the recording head produce a magnetic pattern on the tape. When the tape is played back electrical signals are produced in the replay head and fed to the loudspeaker.

◀ A compact disc player uses lenses and mirrors to reflect a laser beam off the disc surface. The beam reads the pattern of pits on the disc surface.

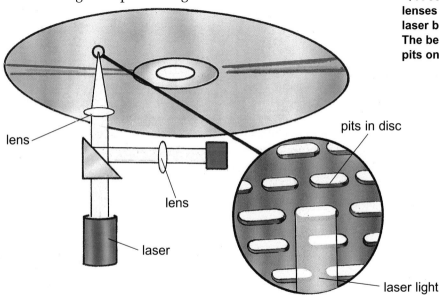

lens

lens

laser

pits in disc

laser light

Milestones

about 1000 Arab scientist Ibn-al-Haitham describes the magnifying glass.

1267 English thinker Roger Bacon describes the magnifying glass.

about 1280 The first mention of a pair of spectacles appears in an Italian book.

about 1590 First microscope is made by Zacharias Janssen in Holland.

1608 Dutch scientist Hans Lippershey invents the lens telescope.

1668 English scientist Isaac Newton invents the reflecting telescope.

1672 Isaac Newton publishes his discoveries about the spectrum.

1690 Dutch physicist Christiaan Huygens puts forward the wave theory of light.

1800 In England, Thomas Young proves the wave theory of light.

1807 The first street lighting is installed in Pall Mall, London.

1822 The first permanent photograph is produced in France by Nicephore Niepce.

1839 The modern photographic process is invented by William Fox Talbot in England.

1877 U.S. inventor Thomas Edison builds the first phonograph to record and play back sounds.

1888 German-American inventor Emile Berliner records sounds on flat disks for the first time.

1900 German physicist Max Planck shows that light consists of units of energy (photons).

1902 Millar Hutchinison invents the first electrical hearing aid in New York.

1960 U.S. physicist Theodore Maiman builds the first laser.

1982 Philips of Holland and Sony of Japan produce the first digital or compact disc.

Glossary

ACOUSTICS   The science that studies sound and hearing.

AMPLIFIER   An electronic device that magnifies the strength of a signal, such as an electrical signal.

AMPLITUDE   The strength of a wave, or the distance from the top of a wave crest to the low point of the wave.

ANALOGUE RECORDING   A recording that stores sound as a continuous signal or pattern. A tape recording, for instance, stores sound as a continuous magnetic pattern on plastic tape.

ANGLE OF INCIDENCE   The angle at which light hits a mirror or enters a transparent material.

ANGLE OF REFLECTION   The angle at which light is reflected from a mirror or smooth surface.

ATOM   A very small particle, the smallest part of a chemical element that takes part in a chemical reaction. Atoms are about a tenth of a millionth of a millimeter across.

COCHLEA   A coiled tube in the inner ear, where vibrations from sound waves are changed into electrical impulses. The impulses are sent to the brain, which interprets them as sounds.

COMPLEMENTARY COLORS   A pair of colors that produce white light when mixed together. Orange and blue are complementary colors, for example.

CONCAVE LENS OR MIRROR   A lens or mirror whose surface is curved inward, like a small cave.

CONVEX LENS OR MIRROR   A lens or mirror that is curved outward. The outside of a shiny spoon forms a convex mirror.

CORNEA   The transparent front part of the eyeball that covers the iris and pupil.

COSMIC RAY   High-energy radiation that reaches the Earth from space.

DECIBEL   A unit used for measuring the loudness of sounds. A soft whisper is close to 0 decibels. A jet taking off is about 120 decibels.

DIFFUSE REFLECTION   The reflection of light from a rough surface which scatters the light in all directions.

DIGITAL RECORDING   A recording that stores sounds or pictures as a pattern of pits or dots representing numbers or digits.

DIRECT LIGHT   Light that comes directly from its source, rather than being reflected off a non-luminous object.

DOPPLER EFFECT   The way the pitch or frequency of waves seems to change if the source of the waves is moving. For example, the pitch of a police car siren seems higher than normal when the car is approaching but lower than normal as the car moves away. The effect is named after the Austrian physicist Christian Doppler (1803-1853).

ECLIPSE When one body in space blocks the light of another body in space. A solar eclipse occurs when the moon temporarily blocks out the light of the sun. A lunar eclipse occurs when the moon passes into the shadow cast by the Earth.

ELECTROMAGNETIC WAVE A wave of electric and magnetic force that can carry energy through empty space. Light, microwaves, ultraviolet rays, infra-red rays, X-rays, and radio waves are all electromagnetic waves with different wavelengths. They all travel through empty space at the same speed, around 186,000 miles (300,000 meters) per second.

ELECTRON A tiny electrically-charged particle that circles the central nucleus of an atom. An electric current is a flow of electrons.

EYEPIECE The small lens of a telescope or microscope nearest the eye.

FOCUS The point at which light rays meet to form a sharp image after passing through a lens, or being reflected from a curved mirror. It is also called the focal point.

FOCAL POINT The same as FOCUS.

FOCAL LENGTH The distance between the focus and the center of the lens or mirror.

FREQUENCY The number of times something is repeated in a set time. In the movement of waves such as radio waves, the frequency of vibrations or peaks in the wave is measured in hertz (the number of cycles per second).

FUNDAMENTAL The simplest vibration or note that a musical instrument can produce.

GAMMA RAY A powerful type of electromagnetic radiation, similar to X-rays, given out when certain atoms disintegrate.

HERTZ The unit used to measure the frequency of a wave or vibration. One hertz is one wave or vibration per second.

ILLUMINATION The brightness or intensity of light falling on a surface. It depends upon the brightness, distance, and angle of any nearby light sources.

IMAGE A picture or appearance of a real object formed by an optical or electronic device. A camera forms an image on the film; our eyes form an image on the retina.

INCANDESCENT OBJECT An object that gives out light because it is very hot. The filament of a light bulb is incandescent.

INDIRECT LIGHT Light that reaches the eye after being reflected off an non-luminous object.

INFRARED RADIATION A type of electromagnetic radiation with a wavelength just longer than that of red light. It can be felt as heat.

IRIS The colored part of the eye

between the clear outer layer (the cornea) and the eye lens. It contains a muscle that opens and closes the pupil to control the amount of light entering the eye.

LASER A device that produces a powerful beam of light. A laser is a light amplifier that increases an initial weak pulse of light into an intense narrow beam. Lasers are used in medicine and industry.

LENS A piece of glass or transparent material that has curved surfaces. Light passing through a lens is bent and can form an image. Lenses are used in cameras, microscopes, and telescopes.

LUMINOUS OBJECT An object that produces light.

MOLECULE The smallest particle of a chemical compound, consisting of one or more atoms combined.

NANOMETER 1 nanometer = 1 thousand millionth of a meter.

OBJECTIVE LENS The front, largest lens in a telescope or microscope.

OPAQUE OBJECT An object that light cannot pass through.

OVERTONE A note that has a frequency or pitch higher than the fundamental frequency, the sounding body's natural frequency.

PENUMBRA The half-dark outer region of a shadow. A large source of light produces shadows that have a penumbra surrounding a smaller dark region called the umbra.

PHOTON A unit of light energy. In some situations, a beam of light behaves as if it were a stream of small particles, which scientists call photons.

PITCH The highness or loudness of a sound. Pitch depends upon the frequency of the sound. The greater the frequency, the higher the pitch.

POLARIZED LIGHT Light in which the wave vibrations are in a definite direction at right angles to the direction of travel of the light.

PRIMARY COLORS Three colors that, when mixed together, can produce any other color. With colored lights, the primary colors are red, green, and blue. With paints, the primary colors are red, yellow, and blue.

PUPIL The hole in the center of the iris in the eye. Light passes through the pupil and falls on the retina at the back of the eye.

REAL IMAGE An image, produced by a lens or mirror, that can be projected onto a screen. A movie projector produces a real image. An image that cannot be projected onto a screen is called a virtual image.

RED SHIFT The color change found in light from the distant galaxies that are moving away from us at great speed. Their light waves are stretched out by their motion and appear redder than normal.

REFRACTION The bending of light rays as they pass from one material to another. Refraction causes a straw in a glass of water to appear bent.

REFRACTIVE INDEX The speed of light in free space divided by the speed of light in a material. The refractive index of water is 1.3.

RETINA The light-sensitive layer at the back of the eyeball.

REVERBERATION The multiple reflections, or echoes, of sounds inside a building that last for a short while before fading away. Reverberations in some buildings can last for a few seconds.

SEISMOGRAPH An instrument for recording the shock waves produced by an earthquake.

SONIC BOOM A loud explosion or bang heard on the ground when a supersonic aircraft passes overhead. It is caused by a shock wave produced by the aircraft.

SPECTRUM The rainbow-colored band of light produced when white light is passed through a prism. The colors are arranged in order of the wavelength of their waves; red is longest and violet is the shortest.

TRANSLUCENT MATERIAL A material that allows some light to pass through but is not transparent. Objects cannot be seen clearly through a translucent material. Tissue paper is translucent.

TRANSPARENT MATERIAL A material that lets light pass through. Objects can be seen clearly though transparent materials. Glass and water are transparent materials.

ULTRASOUND Sound waves of a very high frequency which are beyond human hearing. Ultrasound is used to detect flaws in metals, in medical scanning, depth finding, cleaning, and mixing liquids.

ULTRAVIOLET RADIATION A type of electromagnetic radiation with a wavelength shorter than violet light. Ultraviolet rays occur in sunlight and cause sunburn.

UMBRA The dark inner region of a shadow. A large source of light produces shadows that have an umbra surrounded by a half-dark region called the penumbra.

VIBRATION A quick back and forth movement.

VIRTUAL IMAGE An image that cannot be projected onto a screen. The image seen through a magnifying glass is a virtual image.

WAVELENGTH The distance between successive crests of a wave. The wavelength of a light wave determines its color; red light has a wavelength of about 700 nanometers, for example.

For Further Reading

Ardley, Neil.
Sound Waves to Music: Projects with Sound.
Franklin Watts, Chicago. 1990.

Asimov, Isaac.
How Did We Find Out About Light?
Walker, New York. 1986.

Brandt, Keith.
Sound
Troll, N.J. 1985.

Cash, Terry.
Sound.
Franklin Watts, Chicago. 1989.

Darling, David.
The Science of Acoustics.
Dillon, Minneapolis. 1991.

Devonshire, Hilary.
Light.
Franklin Watts, Chicago. 1992.

Gardner, Robert.
Experimenting with Sound.
Franklin Watts, Chicago. 1992.

Jennings, Terry.
Sounds.
Children's Press, Chicago. 1989.

Kerrod, Robin.
Sounds and Music.
Marshall Cavendish, Tarrytown, N.Y. 1989.

Lampton, Christopher.
Sound: More Than What You Hear.
Enslow, Hillside, N.J. 1992.

MacKinnon, Debbie.
What Noise?
Dial, New York. 1994.

Morgan, Sally.
Using Sound.
Facts on File, New York. 1994.

Zubrowski, Bernie.
Mirrors: Finding Out about the Properties of Light.
Morrow, New York. 1992.

Answers

62

Page 10

Light travels 5,878,000,000,000 miles (9,460,000,000,000 km) in a year.

Page 12

Some luminous objects are: light bulbs, burning candles or matches, neon advertising signs, flashlights, television sets, glow worms, and fireworks.

Page 14
Investigation:

If an object is larger than the light source, its shadow will be larger than its real size. If the object is smaller than the light source, its shadow will be smaller and, if it is the same size, its shadow will be the same size.

At noontime, your shadow is small; late in the afternoon, your shadow is much larger. The size and length of a shadow depends upon the angle at which light strikes the object.

Page 22

A horizontal mirror, such as the surface of a lake, reverses up and down directions because higher objects seem to be further behind the mirror surface than lower objects.

Investigation:

The writing is reversed left to right. The paper has to be positioned with the reversed writing upside down. The mirror reverses the writing left to right and up to down.

Page 24
Investigation:

The paper will melt because the sun's heat is concentrated at the mirror's focus. An image of the window will be seen on the cardboard. To see a clear image, you will have to move the cardboard until it is the correct distance from the mirror. The image is small and upside down.

Page 26
Investigation:

You will see a swirling effect as the sugar solution mixes with the water. Light travels more slowly in the sugar solution than in water. Light rays passing through the jar are bent as they pass through the sugar, producing the swirls.

Page 28
Investigation:

Placing the object closer to the jar than the focus will produce a magnified image seen through the jar.

Investigation:

The magnifying power of the lens is the number of times the image is bigger than the object, or the number of lines outside the lens that fit into one line seen through the lens. A fat lens has a greater magnifying power. A wide lens has the same magnifying power as a smaller lens of the same thickness, but the image may be blurred when seen through the edges of the lens.

Page 30
Investigation:

The image of the scene outside the window is small and upside down. The arrangement is similar to a movie projector.

Page 36

The wavelength of yellow light is about 550 nanometers.

Investigation:

The sunlight is broken into a spectrum as it passes through the water onto the mirror.

Page 38

A blue book looks black in green and red light. It looks blue in blue and white light.

Page 40
Investigation:

The disk with yellow and blue dots appears white when spun. The disk with red and green segments appears yellow when spun.

Page 42

Clatter (falling tin cans), crackle (wood burning on fire), tick (clock), crunch (walking on gravel), bang (door slamming), patter (raindrops falling), tinkle (hitting spoon against drinking glass), rumble (thunder).

Page 46

A mosquito makes a high-pitched sound because it is beating its wings very rapidly (at a high frequency), making many vibrations each second.

Page 48
Investigation:

In the two seconds between claps, the sound travels to the building and back. The time traveled in one second is half this distance, that is, the distance to the building.

Page 50
Investigation:

The stretched wire will produce a musical note when plucked. The shorter the sounding wire, the higher the pitch of the note produced. The greater the weight, the higher the pitch of the note produced.

Page 54
Investigation:

Your nail is being forced to vibrate as it follows the groove. The vibrating nail reproduces the sounds recorded on the record.

Index

(Number in italics refer to illustrations)

acoustics 48, 57
amplifier 54, 57
amplitude 10, 47, 57
analog recording 54, 57
angle of incidence 22, *22*, 57
angle of reflection 22, *22*, 57
anti-noise 53
atom 12, 32, *32*, 57

Bacon Roger 56
Berliner, Émile 56
binoculars 31, *31*
blind spot *16*, 17

chameleon *39*
choroid *16*
cochlea 45, *45*, 57
color 35, 36-37
colorblind test *17*
color mixing 40-41
colored objects 38-39
compact disc 55, *55*, 56
complementary colors 40, 57
convex lens 28, *28*, 29, *29*, 57
concave lens 28, *28*, 29, 57
concave mirror 24, *24*, 25, 57
cone 17
convex mirror 24, 25
cornea 16, *16*, 57
cosmic ray 57

decibel *47*, 57
diffuse reflection 22, 57
digital recording 54, 57
direct light 13, *13*, 57
discharge tube *12*
Doppler effect 53, *53*, 57

ear 45, *45*
echo 48
eclipse 14, 58
Edison, Thomas 56
electromagnetic wave 9, 10, 35, 58
electromagnetic spectrum 10, *10*, 11, 35
electron 12, 58
electronic instruments 51, *51*
eye 16, *16*
eyepiece 30, *30*, 58

far-sightedness 17, *17*
fluorescent lighting 12, *12*
focal length 28, 58
focal point 58
focus 24, 29, *29*, 58

frequency 11, 46, *46*, 50, 58
Fresnel lens *29*
fundamental 51, 58

gamma ray *10*, 11, 58
glow worm 13

hearing aid 56
hertz 11, 58
hologram 32
humpback whale 47
Hutchinson, Millar 56
Huygens, Christiaan 56

Ibn-al-Haitham 56
illumination 14-15, 58
image 23, *23*, *28*, 29, *29*, 30, 58
incandescent object 12, 58
indirect light 13, *13*, 58
infared ray *10*, 11, 58
iris 16, *16*, 58

Janssen, Zacharias 56

laser 21, 32-33, *32*, *33*, 56, 59
lens 21, 28-29, *28*, *29*, 59
light energy 9, *9*
light-year 11
Lippershey, Hans 56
loudness 47, *47*
luminous object 12, 59
lunar eclipse 14

magnifying glass 29, *29*, 56
Maiman, Theodore 56
microscope *20*, 21, 30, *30*, 56
microwaves 10, 11, *11*
mirage 27, *27*
mirror image 23, *23*
mixing colors 44-41
molecule 10, 44, *44*, 59
musical instruments 50, *50*, 51
musical sounds 43, 50-51, *52*

nanometer 37, 59
near-sightedness 17, *17*
Newton, Isaac 9, 35, 36, 56
Niepce, Nicephore 56
noise 43, *52*

objective lens 30, *30*, 59
opaque object 38, 57
optic nerve 16, *16*, 17
overtone 51, 59

penumbra 14, *14*, 15, 59
phonograph 56
photograph 56
photon 9, 13, 32, *32*, 56, 59
pitch 46, 53, *52*
Planck, Max 56
polarized light 18-19, *18*, *19*, 59
primary color 40, *40*, 59

projector 30, *30*
pupil 16, *16*, 59

radar *10*
radio waves 10, *11*
rainbow *34*, 35, 36-37, *36*
real image 30, 59
recording sound 54-55, 56
record player 54, *54*
red shift 53, 59
reflection of light 22-23, *22*, *23*
refraction 26-27, *26*, *27*, 59
refractive index 26, 60
retina 16, *16*, 17, 60
reverberation 49, 60
rod 17

scattering of light 41, *41*
sclera *16*
secondary colors 40, *40*
seismograph 60
shadow 14
soap bubbles *8*
solar eclipse 14
solar power *9*
sonar *48*
sonic boom 52, *52*, 60
sound waves 43, 44, *44*, 46
spectacles 17, 56
spectrum 11, 35, 36, 56, 60
speed of light 10, 11, *11*, 26
speed of sound 47
Sun 13
sunset *35*, 41, *41*
synthesizer 51

Talbot, William Fox 56
tape recorder 54, *55*
telescope 21, 24, *25*, 30, 31, 56
transluscent material 39, 60
transparent material 60
transverse wave 18

ultrasound 49, 60
ultrasonic scan 49, *49*
ultraviolet ray *10*, 11, 12, 60
umbra 14, *14*, 15, 60

vibration 43, 44, 60
virtual image 30, 60

wavelength *8*, 10, 11, 35, 36, 46, 60
white light 36

X-ray *10*, 11

Young, Thomas 56

64